Three-figure tables
for CXC

T0344222

CAMBRIDGE
UNIVERSITY PRESS

University Printing House, Cambridge CB2 8BS, United Kingdom

One Liberty Plaza, 20th Floor, New York, NY 10006, USA

477 Williamstown Road, Port Melbourne, VIC 3207, Australia

314–321, 3rd Floor, Plot 3, Splendor Forum, Jasola District Centre,
New Delhi – 110025, India

79 Anson Road, #06–04/06, Singapore 079906

Cambridge University Press is part of the University of Cambridge.

It furthers the University's mission by disseminating knowledge in the pursuit of
education, learning and research at the highest international levels of excellence.

Information on this title: education.cambridge.org

© Cambridge University Press 1964, 1967, 1974, 1985

Adapted from SMP Elementary Tables (second edition)
This edition first published 1985

40 39 38 37 36 35 34 33 32 31 30 29 28

Printed in Great Britain by Ashford Colour Press Ltd.

ISBN 978-0-521-31453-4 Paperback

Contents

LOGARITHMS

	0	1	2	3	4	5	6	7	8	9
1·0	0·000	004	009	013	017	021	025	029	033	037
1·1	0·041	045	049	053	057	061	064	068	072	076
1·2	0·079	083	086	090	093	097	100	104	107	111
1·3	0·114	117	121	124	127	130	134	137	140	143
1·4	0·146	149	152	155	158	161	164	167	170	173
1·5	0·176	179	182	185	188	190	193	196	199	201
1·6	0·204	207	210	212	215	217	220	223	225	228
1·7	0·230	233	236	238	241	243	246	248	250	253
1·8	0·255	258	260	262	265	267	270	272	274	276
1·9	0·279	281	283	286	288	290	292	294	297	299
2·0	0·301	303	305	307	310	312	314	316	318	320
2·1	0·322	324	326	328	330	332	334	336	338	340
2·2	0·342	344	346	348	350	352	354	356	358	360
2·3	0·362	364	365	367	369	371	373	375	377	378
2·4	0·380	382	384	386	387	389	391	393	394	396
2·5	0·398	400	401	403	405	407	408	410	412	413
2·6	0·415	417	418	420	422	423	425	427	428	430
2·7	0·431	433	435	436	438	439	441	442	444	446
2·8	0·447	449	450	452	453	455	456	458	459	461
2·9	0·462	464	465	467	468	470	471	473	474	476
3·0	0·477	479	480	481	483	484	486	487	489	490
3·1	0·491	493	494	496	497	498	500	501	502	504
3·2	0·505	507	508	509	511	512	513	515	516	517
3·3	0·519	520	521	522	524	525	526	528	529	530
3·4	0·531	533	534	535	537	538	539	540	542	543
3·5	0·544	545	547	548	549	550	551	553	554	555
3·6	0·556	558	559	560	561	562	563	565	566	567
3·7	0·568	569	571	572	573	574	575	576	577	579
3·8	0·580	581	582	583	584	585	587	588	589	590
3·9	0·591	592	593	594	595	597	598	599	600	601
4·0	0·602	603	604	605	606	607	609	610	611	612
4·1	0·613	614	615	616	617	618	619	620	621	622
4·2	0·623	624	625	626	627	628	629	630	631	632
4·3	0·633	634	635	636	637	638	639	640	641	642
4·4	0·643	644	645	646	647	648	649	650	651	652
4·5	0·653	654	655	656	657	658	659	660	661	662
4·6	0·663	664	665	666	667	667	668	669	670	671
4·7	0·672	673	674	675	676	677	678	679	679	680
4·8	0·681	682	683	684	685	686	687	688	688	689
4·9	0·690	691	692	693	694	695	695	696	697	698
5·0	0·699	700	701	702	702	703	704	705	706	707
5·1	0·708	708	709	710	711	712	713	713	714	715
5·2	0·716	717	718	719	719	720	721	722	723	723
5·3	0·724	725	726	727	728	728	729	730	731	732
5·4	0·732	733	734	735	736	736	737	738	739	740

LOGARITHMS

	0	1	2	3	4	5	6	7	8	9
5·5	0·740	741	742	743	744	744	745	746	747	747
5·6	0·748	749	750	751	751	752	753	754	754	755
5·7	0·756	757	757	758	759	760	760	761	762	763
5·8	0·763	764	765	766	766	767	768	769	769	770
5·9	0·771	772	772	773	774	775	775	776	777	777
6·0	0·778	779	780	780	781	782	782	783	784	785
6·1	0·785	786	787	787	788	789	790	790	791	792
6·2	0·792	793	794	794	795	796	797	797	798	799
6·3	0·799	800	801	801	802	803	803	804	805	806
6·4	0·806	807	808	808	809	810	810	811	812	812
6·5	0·813	814	814	815	816	816	817	818	818	819
6·6	0·820	820	821	822	822	823	823	824	825	825
6·7	0·826	827	827	828	829	829	830	831	831	832
6·8	0·833	833	834	834	835	836	836	837	838	838
6·9	0·839	839	840	841	841	842	843	843	844	844
7·0	0·845	846	846	847	848	848	849	849	850	851
7·1	0·851	852	852	853	854	854	855	856	856	857
7·2	0·857	858	859	859	860	860	861	862	862	863
7·3	0·863	864	865	865	866	866	867	867	868	869
7·4	0·869	870	870	871	872	872	873	873	874	874
7·5	0·875	876	876	877	877	878	879	879	880	880
7·6	0·881	881	882	883	883	884	884	885	885	886
7·7	0·886	887	888	888	889	889	890	890	891	892
7·8	0·892	893	893	894	894	895	895	896	897	897
7·9	0·898	898	899	899	900	900	901	901	902	903
8·0	0·903	904	904	905	905	906	906	907	907	908
8·1	0·908	909	910	910	911	911	912	912	913	913
8·2	0·914	914	915	915	916	916	917	918	918	919
8·3	0·919	920	920	921	921	922	922	923	923	924
8·4	0·924	925	925	926	926	927	927	928	928	929
8·5	0·929	930	930	931	931	932	932	933	933	934
8·6	0·934	935	936	936	937	937	938	938	939	939
8·7	0·940	940	941	941	942	942	943	943	943	944
8·8	0·944	945	945	946	946	947	947	948	948	949
8·9	0·949	950	950	951	951	952	952	953	953	954
9·0	0·954	955	955	956	956	957	957	958	958	959
9·1	0·959	960	960	960	961	961	962	962	963	963
9·2	0·964	964	965	965	966	966	967	967	968	968
9·3	0·968	969	969	970	970	971	971	972	972	973
9·4	0·973	974	974	975	975	975	976	976	977	977
9·5	0·978	978	979	979	980	980	980	981	981	982
9·6	0·982	983	983	984	984	985	985	985	986	986
9·7	0·987	987	988	988	989	989	989	990	990	991
9·8	0·991	992	992	993	993	993	994	994	995	995
9·9	0·996	996	997	997	997	998	998	999	999	1·000
10·0	1·000									

ANTI-LOGARITHMS

	0	1	2	3	4	5	6	7	8	9
0·00	100	100	100	101	101	101	101	102	102	102
0·01	102	103	103	103	103	104	104	104	104	104
0·02	105	105	105	105	106	106	106	106	107	107
0·03	107	107	108	108	108	108	109	109	109	109
0·04	110	110	110	110	111	111	111	111	112	112
0·05	112	112	113	113	113	114	114	114	114	115
0·06	115	115	115	116	116	116	116	117	117	117
0·07	117	118	118	118	119	119	119	119	120	120
0·08	120	120	121	121	121	122	122	122	122	123
0·09	123	123	124	124	124	124	125	125	125	126
0·10	126	126	126	127	127	127	128	128	128	129
0·11	129	129	129	130	130	130	131	131	131	132
0·12	132	132	132	133	133	133	134	134	134	135
0·13	135	135	136	136	136	136	137	137	137	138
0·14	138	138	139	139	139	140	140	140	141	141
0·15	141	142	142	142	143	143	143	144	144	144
0·16	145	145	145	146	146	146	147	147	147	148
0·17	148	148	149	149	149	150	150	150	151	151
0·18	151	152	152	152	153	153	153	154	154	155
0·19	155	155	156	156	156	157	157	157	158	158
0·20	158	159	159	160	160	160	161	161	161	162
0·21	162	163	163	163	164	164	164	165	165	166
0·22	166	166	167	167	167	168	168	169	169	169
0·23	170	170	171	171	171	172	172	173	173	173
0·24	174	174	175	175	175	176	176	177	177	177
0·25	178	178	179	179	179	180	180	181	181	182
0·26	182	182	183	183	184	184	184	185	185	186
0·27	186	187	187	188	188	188	189	189	190	190
0·28	191	191	191	192	192	193	193	194	194	195
0·29	195	195	196	196	197	197	198	198	199	199
0·30	200	200	200	201	201	202	202	203	203	204
0·31	204	205	205	206	206	207	207	207	208	208
0·32	209	209	210	210	211	211	212	212	213	213
0·33	214	214	215	215	216	216	217	217	218	218
0·34	219	219	220	220	221	221	222	222	223	223
0·35	224	224	225	225	226	226	227	228	228	229
0·36	229	230	230	231	231	232	232	233	233	234
0·37	234	235	236	236	237	237	238	238	239	239
0·38	240	240	241	242	242	243	243	244	244	245
0·39	245	246	247	247	248	248	249	249	250	251
0·40	251	252	252	253	254	254	255	255	256	256
0·41	257	258	258	259	259	260	261	261	262	262
0·42	263	264	264	265	265	266	267	267	268	269
0·43	269	270	270	271	272	272	273	274	274	275
0·44	275	276	277	277	278	279	279	280	281	281
0·45	282	282	283	284	284	285	286	286	287	288
0·46	288	289	290	290	291	292	292	293	294	294
0·47	295	296	296	297	298	299	299	300	301	301
0·48	302	303	303	304	305	305	306	307	308	308
0·49	309	310	310	311	312	313	313	314	315	316

ANTI-LOGARITHMS

	0	1	2	3	4	5	6	7	8	9
0·50	316	317	318	318	319	320	321	321	322	323
0·51	324	324	325	326	327	327	328	329	330	330
0·52	331	332	333	333	334	335	336	337	337	338
0·53	339	340	340	341	342	343	344	344	345	346
0·54	347	348	348	349	350	351	352	352	353	354
0·55	355	356	356	357	358	359	360	361	361	362
0·56	363	364	365	366	366	367	368	369	370	371
0·57	372	372	373	374	375	376	377	378	378	379
0·58	380	381	382	383	384	385	385	386	387	388
0·59	389	390	391	392	393	394	394	395	396	397
0·60	398	399	400	401	402	403	404	405	406	406
0·61	407	408	409	410	411	412	413	414	415	416
0·62	417	418	419	420	421	422	423	424	425	426
0·63	427	428	429	430	431	432	433	434	435	436
0·64	437	438	439	440	441	442	443	444	445	446
0·65	447	448	449	450	451	452	453	454	455	456
0·66	457	458	459	460	461	462	463	465	466	467
0·67	468	469	470	471	472	473	474	475	476	478
0·68	479	480	481	482	483	484	485	486	488	489
0·69	490	491	492	493	494	495	497	498	499	500
0·70	501	502	504	505	506	507	508	509	510	512
0·71	513	514	515	516	518	519	520	521	522	524
0·72	525	526	527	528	530	531	532	533	535	536
0·73	537	538	540	541	542	543	544	546	547	548
0·74	550	551	552	553	555	556	557	558	560	561
0·75	562	564	565	566	568	569	570	571	573	574
0·76	575	577	578	579	581	582	583	585	586	587
0·77	589	590	591	593	594	596	597	598	600	601
0·78	603	604	605	607	608	610	611	612	614	615
0·79	617	618	619	621	622	624	625	627	628	630
0·80	631	632	634	635	637	638	640	641	643	644
0·81	646	647	649	650	652	653	655	656	658	659
0·82	661	662	664	665	667	668	670	671	673	675
0·83	676	678	679	681	682	684	685	687	689	690
0·84	692	693	695	697	698	700	701	703	705	706
0·85	708	710	711	713	714	716	718	719	721	723
0·86	724	726	728	729	731	733	735	736	738	740
0·87	741	743	745	746	748	750	752	753	755	757
0·88	759	760	762	764	766	767	769	771	773	774
0·89	776	778	780	782	783	785	787	789	791	792
0·90	794	796	798	800	802	804	805	807	809	811
0·91	813	815	817	818	820	822	824	826	828	830
0·92	832	834	836	838	839	841	843	845	847	849
0·93	851	853	855	857	859	861	863	865	867	869
0·94	871	873	875	877	879	881	883	885	887	889
0·95	891	893	895	897	900	902	904	906	908	910
0·96	912	914	916	918	920	923	925	927	929	931
0·97	933	935	938	940	942	944	946	948	951	953
0·98	955	957	959	962	964	966	968	971	973	975
0·99	977	979	982	984	986	989	991	993	995	998

SINES

$r \sin \theta$

Angle in degrees	·0	·1	·2	·3	·4	·5	·6	·7	·8	·9
0	0·000	·002	·003	·005	·007	·009	·010	·012	·014	·016
1	0·017	·019	·021	·023	·024	·026	·028	·030	·031	·033
2	0·035	·037	·038	·040	·042	·044	·045	·047	·049	·051
3	0·052	·054	·056	·058	·059	·061	·063	·065	·066	·068
4	0·070	·071	·073	·075	·077	·078	·080	·082	·084	·085
5	0·087	·089	·091	·092	·094	·096	·098	·099	·101	·103
6	0·105	·106	·108	·110	·111	·113	·115	·117	·118	·120
7	0·122	·124	·125	·127	·129	·131	·132	·134	·136	·137
8	0·139	·141	·143	·144	·146	·148	·150	·151	·153	·155
9	0·156	·158	·160	·162	·163	·165	·167	·168	·170	·172
10	0·174	·175	·177	·179	·181	·182	·184	·186	·187	·189
11	0·191	·193	·194	·196	·198	·199	·201	·203	·204	·206
12	0·208	·210	·211	·213	·215	·216	·218	·220	·222	·223
13	0·225	·227	·228	·230	·232	·233	·235	·237	·239	·240
14	0·242	·244	·245	·247	·249	·250	·252	·254	·255	·257
15	0·259	·261	·262	·264	·266	·267	·269	·271	·272	·274
16	0·276	·277	·279	·281	·282	·284	·286	·287	·289	·291
17	0·292	·294	·296	·297	·299	·301	·302	·304	·306	·307
18	0·309	·311	·312	·314	·316	·317	·319	·321	·322	·324
19	0·326	·327	·329	·331	·332	·334	·335	·337	·339	·340
20	0·342	·344	·345	·347	·349	·350	·352	·353	·355	·357
21	0·358	·360	·362	·363	·365	·367	·368	·370	·371	·373
22	0·375	·376	·378	·379	·381	·383	·384	·386	·388	·389
23	0·391	·392	·394	·396	·397	·399	·400	·402	·404	·405
24	0·407	·408	·410	·412	·413	·415	·416	·418	·419	·421
25	0·423	·424	·426	·427	·429	·431	·432	·434	·435	·437
26	0·438	·440	·442	·443	·445	·446	·448	·449	·451	·452
27	0·454	·456	·457	·459	·460	·462	·463	·465	·466	·468
28	0·469	·471	·473	·474	·476	·477	·479	·480	·482	·483
29	0·485	·486	·488	·489	·491	·492	·494	·495	·497	·498
30	0·500	·502	·503	·505	·506	·508	·509	·511	·512	·514
31	0·515	·517	·518	·520	·521	·522	·524	·525	·527	·528
32	0·530	·531	·533	·534	·536	·537	·539	·540	·542	·543
33	0·545	·546	·548	·549	·550	·552	·553	·555	·556	·558
34	0·559	·561	·562	·564	·565	·566	·568	·569	·571	·572
35	0·574	·575	·576	·578	·579	·581	·582	·584	·585	·586
36	0·588	·589	·591	·592	·593	·595	·596	·598	·599	·600
37	0·602	·603	·605	·606	·607	·609	·610	·612	·613	·614
38	0·616	·617	·618	·620	·621	·623	·624	·625	·627	·628
39	0·629	·631	·632	·633	·635	·636	·637	·639	·640	·641
40	0·643	·644	·645	·647	·648	·649	·651	·652	·653	·655
41	0·656	·657	·659	·660	·661	·663	·664	·665	·667	·668
42	0·669	·670	·672	·673	·674	·676	·677	·678	·679	·681
43	0·682	·683	·685	·686	·687	·688	·690	·691	·692	·693
44	0·695	·696	·697	·698	·700	·701	·702	·703	·705	·706
45	0·707	·708	·710	·711	·712	·713	·714	·716	·717	·718

If, for small values of the angle (up to about 6°), more figures are required than are given in the table, they can be obtained from the formula

$$\sin (\theta°) \approx 0·01745\,\theta.$$

SINES

Angle in degrees	·0	·1	·2	·3	·4	·5	·6	·7	·8	·9
45	0·707	·708	·710	·711	·712	·713	·714	·716	·717	·718
46	0·719	·721	·722	·723	·724	·725	·727	·728	·729	·730
47	0·731	·733	·734	·735	·736	·737	·738	·740	·741	·742
48	0·743	·744	·745	·747	·748	·749	·750	·751	·752	·754
49	0·755	·756	·757	·758	·759	·760	·762	·763	·764	·765
50	0·766	·767	·768	·769	·771	·772	·773	·774	·775	·776
51	0·777	·778	·779	·780	·782	·783	·784	·785	·786	·787
52	0·788	·789	·790	·791	·792	·793	·794	·795	·797	·798
53	0·799	·800	·801	·802	·803	·804	·805	·806	·807	·808
54	0·809	·810	·811	·812	·813	·814	·815	·816	·817	·818
55	0·819	·820	·821	·822	·823	·824	·825	·826	·827	·828
56	0·829	·830	·831	·832	·833	·834	·835	·836	·837	·838
57	0·839	·840	·841	·842	·842	·843	·844	·845	·846	·847
58	0·848	·849	·850	·851	·852	·853	·854	·854	·855	·856
59	0·857	·858	·859	·860	·861	·862	·863	·863	·864	·865
60	0·866	·867	·868	·869	·869	·870	·871	·872	·873	·874
61	0·875	·875	·876	·877	·878	·879	·880	·880	·881	·882
62	0·883	·884	·885	·885	·886	·887	·888	·889	·889	·890
63	0·891	·892	·893	·893	·894	·895	·896	·896	·897	·898
64	0·899	·900	·900	·901	·902	·903	·903	·904	·905	·906
65	0·906	·907	·908	·909	·909	·910	·911	·911	·912	·913
66	0·914	·914	·915	·916	·916	·917	·918	·918	·919	·920
67	0·921	·921	·922	·923	·923	·924	·925	·925	·926	·927
68	0·927	·928	·928	·929	·930	·930	·931	·932	·932	·933
69	0·934	·934	·935	·935	·936	·937	·937	·938	·938	·939
70	0·940	·940	·941	·941	·942	·943	·943	·944	·944	·945
71	0·946	·946	·947	·947	·948	·948	·949	·949	·950	·951
72	0·951	·952	·952	·953	·953	·954	·954	·955	·955	·956
73	0·956	·957	·957	·958	·958	·959	·959	·960	·960	·961
74	0·961	·962	·962	·963	·963	·964	·964	·965	·965	·965
75	0·966	·966	·967	·967	·968	·968	·969	·969	·969	·970
76	0·970	·971	·971	·972	·972	·972	·973	·973	·974	·974
77	0·974	·975	·975	·976	·976	·976	·977	·977	·977	·978
78	0·978	·979	·979	·979	·980	·980	·980	·981	·981	·981
79	0·982	·982	·982	·983	·983	·983	·984	·984	·984	·985
80	0·985	·985	·985	·986	·986	·986	·987	·987	·987	·987
81	0·988	·988	·988	·988	·989	·989	·989	·990	·990	·990
82	0·990	·991	·991	·991	·991	·991	·992	·992	·992	·992
83	0·993	·993	·993	·993	·993	·994	·994	·994	·994	·994
84	0·995	·995	·995	·995	·995	·995	·996	·996	·996	·996
85	0·996	·996	·996	·997	·997	·997	·997	·997	·997	·997
86	0·998	·998	·998	·998	·998	·998	·998	·998	·998	·999
87	0·999	·999	·999	·999	·999	·999	·999	·999	·999	·999
88	0·999	·999	1·000	1·000	1·000	1·000	1·000	1·000	1·000	1·000
89	1·000	1·000	1·000	1·000	1·000	1·000	1·000	1·000	1·000	1·000
90	1·000									

COSINES

$r \cos \theta$

Angle in degrees	·0	·1	·2	·3	·4	·5	·6	·7	·8	·9
0	1·000	1·000	1·000	1·000	1·000	1·000	1·000	1·000	1·000	1·000
1	1·000	1·000	1·000	1·000	1·000	1·000	1·000	1·000	1·000	0·999
2	0·999	·999	·999	·999	·999	·999	·999	·999	·999	·999
3	0·999	·999	·998	·998	·998	·998	·998	·998	·998	·998
4	0·998	·997	·997	·997	·997	·997	·997	·997	·996	·996
5	0·996	·996	·996	·996	·996	·995	·995	·995	·995	·995
6	0·995	·994	·994	·994	·994	·994	·993	·993	·993	·993
7	0·993	·992	·992	·992	·992	·991	·991	·991	·991	·991
8	0·990	·990	·990	·990	·989	·989	·989	·988	·988	·988
9	0·988	·987	·987	·987	·987	·986	·986	·986	·985	·985
10	0·985	·985	·984	·984	·984	·983	·983	·983	·982	·982
11	0·982	·981	·981	·981	·980	·980	·980	·979	·979	·979
12	0·978	·978	·977	·977	·977	·976	·976	·976	·975	·975
13	0·974	·974	·974	·973	·973	·972	·972	·972	·971	·971
14	0·970	·970	·969	·969	·969	·968	·968	·967	·967	·966
15	0·966	·965	·965	·965	·964	·964	·963	·963	·962	·962
16	0·961	·961	·960	·960	·959	·959	·958	·958	·957	·957
17	0·956	·956	·955	·955	·954	·954	·953	·953	·952	·952
18	0·951	·951	·950	·949	·949	·948	·948	·947	·947	·946
19	0·946	·945	·944	·944	·943	·943	·942	·941	·941	·940
20	0·940	·939	·938	·938	·937	·937	·936	·935	·935	·934
21	0·934	·933	·932	·932	·931	·930	·930	·929	·928	·928
22	0·927	·927	·926	·925	·925	·924	·923	·923	·922	·921
23	0·921	·920	·919	·918	·918	·917	·916	·916	·915	·914
24	0·914	·913	·912	·911	·911	·910	·909	·909	·908	·907
25	0·906	·906	·905	·904	·903	·903	·902	·901	·900	·900
26	0·899	·898	·897	·896	·896	·895	·894	·893	·893	·892
27	0·891	·890	·889	·889	·888	·887	·886	·885	·885	·884
28	0·883	·882	·881	·880	·880	·879	·878	·877	·876	·875
29	0·875	·874	·873	·872	·871	·870	·869	·869	·868	·867
30	0·866	·865	·864	·863	·863	·862	·861	·860	·859	·858
31	0·857	·856	·855	·854	·854	·853	·852	·851	·850	·849
32	0·848	·847	·846	·845	·844	·843	·842	·842	·841	·840
33	0·839	·838	·837	·836	·835	·834	·833	·832	·831	·830
34	0·829	·828	·827	·826	·825	·824	·823	·822	·821	·820
35	0·819	·818	·817	·816	·815	·814	·813	·812	·811	·810
36	0·809	·808	·807	·806	·805	·804	·803	·802	·801	·800
37	0·799	·798	·797	·795	·794	·793	·792	·791	·790	·789
38	0·788	·787	·786	·785	·784	·783	·782	·780	·779	·778
39	0·777	·776	·775	·774	·773	·772	·771	·769	·768	·767
40	0·766	·765	·764	·763	·762	·760	·759	·758	·757	·756
41	0·755	·754	·752	·751	·750	·749	·748	·747	·745	·744
42	0·743	·742	·741	·740	·738	·737	·736	·735	·734	·733
43	0·731	·730	·729	·728	·727	·725	·724	·723	·722	·721
44	0·719	·718	·717	·716	·714	·713	·712	·711	·710	·708
45	0·707	·706	·705	·703	·702	·701	·700	·698	·697	·696

COSINES

$r \cos \theta$

Angle in degrees	·0	·1	·2	·3	·4	·5	·6	·7	·8	·9
45	0·707	·706	·705	·703	·702	·701	·700	·698	·697	·696
46	0·695	·693	·692	·691	·690	·688	·687	·686	·685	·683
47	0·682	·681	·679	·678	·677	·676	·674	·673	·672	·670
48	0·669	·668	·667	·665	·664	·663	·661	·660	·659	·657
49	0·656	·655	·653	·652	·651	·649	·648	·647	·645	·644
50	0·643	·641	·640	·639	·637	·636	·635	·633	·632	·631
51	0·629	·628	·627	·625	·624	·623	·621	·620	·618	·617
52	0·616	·614	·613	·612	·610	·609	·607	·606	·605	·603
53	0·602	·600	·599	·598	·596	·595	·593	·592	·591	·589
54	0·588	·586	·585	·584	·582	·581	·579	·578	·576	·575
55	0·574	·572	·571	·569	·568	·566	·565	·564	·562	·561
56	0·559	·558	·556	·555	·553	·552	·550	·549	·548	·546
57	0·545	·543	·542	·540	·539	·537	·536	·534	·533	·531
58	0·530	·528	·527	·525	·524	·522	·521	·520	·518	·517
59	0·515	·514	·512	·511	·509	·508	·506	·505	·503	·502
60	0·500	·498	·497	·495	·494	·492	·491	·489	·488	·486
61	0·485	·483	·482	·480	·479	·477	·476	·474	·473	·471
62	0·469	·468	·466	·465	·463	·462	·460	·459	·457	·456
63	0·454	·452	·451	·449	·448	·446	·445	·443	·442	·440
64	0·438	·437	·435	·434	·432	·431	·429	·427	·426	·424
65	0·423	·421	·419	·418	·416	·415	·413	·412	·410	·408
66	0·407	·405	·404	·402	·400	·399	·397	·396	·394	·392
67	0·391	·389	·388	·386	·384	·383	·381	·379	·378	·376
68	0·375	·373	·371	·370	·368	·367	·365	·363	·362	·360
69	0·358	·357	·355	·353	·352	·350	·349	·347	·345	·344
70	0·342	·340	·339	·337	·335	·334	·332	·331	·329	·327
71	0·326	·324	·322	·321	·319	·317	·316	·314	·312	·311
72	0·309	·307	·306	·304	·302	·301	·299	·297	·296	·294
73	0·292	·291	·289	·287	·286	·284	·282	·281	·279	·277
74	0·276	·274	·272	·271	·269	·267	·266	·264	·262	·261
75	0·259	·257	·255	·254	·252	·250	·249	·247	·245	·244
76	0·242	·240	·239	·237	·235	·233	·232	·230	·228	·227
77	0·225	·223	·222	·220	·218	·216	·215	·213	·211	·210
78	0·208	·206	·204	·203	·201	·199	·198	·196	·194	·193
79	0·191	·189	·187	·186	·184	·182	·181	·179	·177	·175
80	0·174	·172	·170	·168	·167	·165	·163	·162	·160	·158
81	0·156	·155	·153	·151	·150	·148	·146	·144	·143	·141
82	0·139	·137	·136	·134	·132	·131	·129	·127	·125	·124
83	0·122	·120	·118	·117	·115	·113	·111	·110	·108	·106
84	0·105	·103	·101	·099	·098	·096	·094	·092	·091	·089
85	0·087	·085	·084	·082	·080	·078	·077	·075	·073	·071
86	0·070	·068	·066	·065	·063	·061	·059	·058	·056	·054
87	0·052	·051	·049	·047	·045	·044	·042	·040	·038	·037
88	0·035	·033	·031	·030	·028	·026	·024	·023	·021	·019
89	0·017	·016	·014	·012	·010	·009	·007	·005	·003	·002
90	0·000									

TANGENTS

Angle in degrees	·0	·1	·2	·3	·4	·5	·6	·7	·8	·9
0	0·000	·002	·003	·005	·007	·009	·010	·012	·014	·016
1	0·017	·019	·021	·023	·024	·026	·028	·030	·031	·033
2	0·035	·037	·038	·040	·042	·044	·045	·047	·049	·051
3	0·052	·054	·056	·058	·059	·061	·063	·065	·066	·068
4	0·070	·072	·073	·075	·077	·079	·080	·082	·084	·086
5	0·087	·089	·091	·093	·095	·096	·098	·100	·102	·103
6	0·105	·107	·109	·110	·112	·114	·116	·117	·119	·121
7	0·123	·125	·126	·128	·130	·132	·133	·135	·137	·139
8	0·141	·142	·144	·146	·148	·149	·151	·153	·155	·157
9	0·158	·160	·162	·164	·166	·167	·169	·171	·173	·175
10	0·176	·178	·180	·182	·184	·185	·187	·189	·191	·193
11	0·194	·196	·198	·200	·202	·203	·205	·207	·209	·211
12	0·213	·214	·216	·218	·220	·222	·224	·225	·227	·229
13	0·231	·233	·235	·236	·238	·240	·242	·244	·246	·247
14	0·249	·251	·253	·255	·257	·259	·260	·262	·264	·266
15	0·268	·270	·272	·274	·275	·277	·279	·281	·283	·285
16	0·287	·289	·291	·292	·294	·296	·298	·300	·302	·304
17	0·306	·308	·310	·311	·313	·315	·317	·319	·321	·323
18	0·325	·327	·329	·331	·333	·335	·337	·338	·340	·342
19	0·344	·346	·348	·350	·352	·354	·356	·358	·360	·362
20	0·364	·366	·368	·370	·372	·374	·376	·378	·380	·382
21	0·384	·386	·388	·390	·392	·394	·396	·398	·400	·402
22	0·404	·406	·408	·410	·412	·414	·416	·418	·420	·422
23	0·424	·427	·429	·431	·433	·435	·437	·439	·441	·443
24	0·445	·447	·449	·452	·454	·456	·458	·460	·462	·464
25	0·466	·468	·471	·473	·475	·477	·479	·481	·483	·486
26	0·488	·490	·492	·494	·496	·499	·501	·503	·505	·507
27	0·510	·512	·514	·516	·518	·521	·523	·525	·527	·529
28	0·532	·534	·536	·538	·541	·543	·545	·547	·550	·552
29	0·554	·557	·559	·561	·563	·566	·568	·570	·573	·575
30	0·577	·580	·582	·584	·587	·589	·591	·594	·596	·598
31	0·601	·603	·606	·608	·610	·613	·615	·618	·620	·622
32	0·625	·627	·630	·632	·635	·637	·640	·642	·644	·647
33	0·649	·652	·654	·657	·659	·662	·664	·667	·669	·672
34	0·675	·677	·680	·682	·685	·687	·690	·692	·695	·698
35	0·700	·703	·705	·708	·711	·713	·716	·719	·721	·724
36	0·727	·729	·732	·735	·737	·740	·743	·745	·748	·751
37	0·754	·756	·759	·762	·765	·767	·770	·773	·776	·778
38	0·781	·784	·787	·790	·793	·795	·798	·801	·804	·807
39	0·810	·813	·816	·818	·821	·824	·827	·830	·833	·836
40	0·839	·842	·845	·848	·851	·854	·857	·860	·863	·866
41	0·869	·872	·875	·879	·882	·885	·888	·891	·894	·897
42	0·900	·904	·907	·910	·913	·916	·920	·923	·926	·929
43	0·933	·936	·939	·942	·946	·949	·952	·956	·959	·962
44	0·966	·969	·972	·976	·979	·983	·986	·990	·993	·997
45	1·00	1·00	1·01	1·01	1·01	1·02	1·02	1·02	1·03	1·03

If, for small values of the angle (up to about 4°), more figures are required than are given in the table, they can be obtained from the formula

$$\tan (\theta°) \approx 0·01746\theta.$$

TANGENTS

Angle in degrees	·0	·1	·2	·3	·4	·5	·6	·7	·8	·9
45	1·00	1·00	1·01	1·01	1·01	1·02	1·02	1·02	1·03	1·03
46	1·04	1·04	1·04	1·05	1·05	1·05	1·06	1·06	1·06	1·07
47	1·07	1·08	1·08	1·08	1·09	1·09	1·10	1·10	1·10	1·11
48	1·11	1·11	1·12	1·12	1·13	1·13	1·13	1·14	1·14	1·15
49	1·15	1·15	1·16	1·16	1·17	1·17	1·17	1·18	1·18	1·19
50	1·19	1·20	1·20	1·20	1·21	1·21	1·22	1·22	1·23	1·23
51	1·23	1·24	1·24	1·25	1·25	1·26	1·26	1·27	1·27	1·28
52	1·28	1·28	1·29	1·29	1·30	1·30	1·31	1·31	1·32	1·32
53	1·33	1·33	1·34	1·34	1·35	1·35	1·36	1·36	1·37	1·37
54	1·38	1·38	1·39	1·39	1·40	1·40	1·41	1·41	1·42	1·42
55	1·43	1·43	1·44	1·44	1·45	1·46	1·46	1·47	1·47	1·48
56	1·48	1·49	1·49	1·50	1·51	1·51	1·52	1·52	1·53	1·53
57	1·54	1·55	1·55	1·56	1·56	1·57	1·58	1·58	1·59	1·59
58	1·60	1·61	1·61	1·62	1·63	1·63	1·64	1·64	1·65	1·66
59	1·66	1·67	1·68	1·68	1·69	1·70	1·70	1·71	1·72	1·73
60	1·73	1·74	1·75	1·75	1·76	1·77	1·77	1·78	1·79	1·80
61	1·80	1·81	1·82	1·83	1·83	1·84	1·85	1·86	1·86	1·87
62	1·88	1·89	1·90	1·90	1·91	1·92	1·93	1·94	1·95	1·95
63	1·96	1·97	1·98	1·99	2·00	2·01	2·01	2·02	2·03	2·04
64	2·05	2·06	2·07	2·08	2·09	2·10	2·11	2·12	2·13	2·13
65	2·14	2·15	2·16	2·17	2·18	2·19	2·20	2·21	2·23	2·24
66	2·25	2·26	2·27	2·28	2·29	2·30	2·31	2·32	2·33	2·34
67	2·36	2·37	2·38	2·39	2·40	2·41	2·43	2·44	2·45	2·46
68	2·48	2·49	2·50	2·51	2·53	2·54	2·55	2·56	2·58	2·59
69	2·61	2·62	2·63	2·65	2·66	2·67	2·69	2·70	2·72	2·73
70	2·75	2·76	2·78	2·79	2·81	2·82	2·84	2·86	2·87	2·89
71	2·90	2·92	2·94	2·95	2·97	2·99	3·01	3·02	3·04	3·06
72	3·08	3·10	3·11	3·13	3·15	3·17	3·19	3·21	3·23	3·25
73	3·27	3·29	3·31	3·33	3·35	3·38	3·40	3·42	3·44	3·46
74	3·49	3·51	3·53	3·56	3·58	3·61	3·63	3·66	3·68	3·71
75	3·73	3·76	3·78	3·81	3·84	3·87	3·89	3·92	3·95	3·98
76	4·01	4·04	4·07	4·10	4·13	4·17	4·20	4·23	4·26	4·30
77	4·33	4·37	4·40	4·44	4·47	4·51	4·55	4·59	4·63	4·66
78	4·70	4·75	4·79	4·83	4·87	4·92	4·96	5·00	5·05	5·10
79	5·14	5·19	5·24	5·29	5·34	5·40	5·45	5·50	5·56	5·61
80	5·67	5·73	5·79	5·85	5·91	5·98	6·04	6·11	6·17	6·24
81	6·31	6·39	6·46	6·54	6·61	6·69	6·77	6·85	6·94	7·03
82	7·12	7·21	7·30	7·40	7·49	7·60	7·70	7·81	7·92	8·03
83	8·14	8·26	8·39	8·51	8·64	8·78	8·92	9·06	9·21	9·36
84	9·51	9·68	9·84	10·0	10·2	10·4	10·6	10·8	11·0	11·2
85	11·4	11·7	11·9	12·2	12·4	12·7	13·0	13·3	13·6	14·0
86	14·3	14·7	15·1	15·5	15·9	16·3	16·8	17·3	17·9	18·5
87	19·1	19·7	20·4	21·2	22·0	22·9	23·9	24·9	26·0	27·3
88	28·6	30·1	31·8	33·7	35·8	38·2	40·9	44·1	47·7	52·1
89	57·3	63·7	71·6	81·8	95·5	115	143	191	286	573

LOGARITHMS OF SINES

	0.0° 0′	0.1° 6′	0.2° 12′	0.3° 18′	0.4° 24′	0.5° 30′	0.6° 36′	0.7° 42′	0.8° 48′	0.9° 54′
0°	$-\infty$	$\bar{3}\cdot242$	$\bar{3}\cdot543$	$\bar{3}\cdot719$	$\bar{3}\cdot844$	$\bar{3}\cdot941$	$\bar{2}\cdot020$	$\bar{2}\cdot087$	$\bar{2}\cdot145$	$\bar{2}\cdot196$
1	$\bar{2}\cdot242$	283	321	356	388	418	446	472	497	521
2	$\bar{2}\cdot543$	564	584	603	622	640	657	673	689	704
3	$\bar{2}\cdot719$	733	747	760	773	786	798	810	821	833
4	$\bar{2}\cdot843$	854	865	875	885	895	904	913	923	932
5	$\bar{2}\cdot940$	949	957	966	974	982	989	997	**005**	**012**
6	$\bar{1}\cdot019$	026	033	040	047	054	060	067	073	080
7	$\bar{1}\cdot086$	092	098	104	110	116	121	127	133	138
8	$\bar{1}\cdot144$	149	154	159	165	170	175	180	185	190
9	$\bar{1}\cdot194$	199	204	208	213	218	222	227	231	235
10	$\bar{1}\cdot240$	244	248	252	257	261	265	269	273	277
11	$\bar{1}\cdot281$	284	288	292	296	300	303	307	311	314
12	$\bar{1}\cdot318$	321	325	328	332	335	339	342	345	349
13	$\bar{1}\cdot352$	355	359	362	365	368	371	374	378	381
14	$\bar{1}\cdot384$	387	390	393	396	399	402	404	407	410
15	$\bar{1}\cdot413$	416	419	421	424	427	430	432	435	438
16	$\bar{1}\cdot440$	443	446	448	451	453	456	458	461	463
17	$\bar{1}\cdot466$	468	471	473	476	478	481	483	485	488
18	$\bar{1}\cdot490$	492	495	497	499	501	504	506	508	510
19	$\bar{1}\cdot513$	515	517	519	521	523	526	528	530	532
20	$\bar{1}\cdot534$	536	538	540	542	544	546	548	550	552
21	$\bar{1}\cdot554$	556	558	560	562	564	566	568	570	572
22	$\bar{1}\cdot574$	575	577	579	581	583	585	586	588	590
23	$\bar{1}\cdot592$	594	595	597	599	601	602	604	606	608
24	$\bar{1}\cdot609$	611	613	614	616	618	619	621	623	624
25	$\bar{1}\cdot626$	628	629	631	632	634	636	637	639	640
26	$\bar{1}\cdot642$	643	645	646	648	650	651	653	654	656
27	$\bar{1}\cdot657$	659	660	661	663	664	666	667	669	670
28	$\bar{1}\cdot672$	673	674	676	677	678	680	681	683	684
29	$\bar{1}\cdot686$	687	688	690	691	692	694	695	696	698
30	$\bar{1}\cdot699$	700	702	703	704	705	707	708	709	711
31	$\bar{1}\cdot712$	713	714	716	717	718	719	721	722	723
32	$\bar{1}\cdot724$	725	727	728	729	730	731	733	734	735
33	$\bar{1}\cdot736$	737	738	740	741	742	743	744	745	746
34	$\bar{1}\cdot748$	749	750	751	752	753	754	755	756	758
35	$\bar{1}\cdot759$	760	761	762	763	764	765	766	767	768
36	$\bar{1}\cdot769$	770	771	772	773	774	775	776	777	778
37	$\bar{1}\cdot779$	780	781	782	783	784	785	786	787	788
38	$\bar{1}\cdot789$	790	791	792	793	794	795	796	797	798
39	$\bar{1}\cdot799$	800	801	802	803	804	804	805	806	807
40	$\bar{1}\cdot808$	809	810	811	812	813	813	814	815	816
41	$\bar{1}\cdot817$	818	819	820	820	821	822	823	824	825
42	$\bar{1}\cdot826$	826	827	828	829	830	831	831	832	833
43	$\bar{1}\cdot834$	835	835	836	837	838	839	839	840	841
44	$\bar{1}\cdot842$	843	843	844	845	846	846	847	848	849

The **bold** type indicates that the integer changes.

LOGARITHMS OF SINES

	0.0° 0′	0.1° 6′	0.2° 12′	0.3° 18′	0.4° 24′	0.5° 30′	0.6° 36′	0.7° 42′	0.8° 48′	0.9° 54′
45°	$\bar{1}$·849	850	851	852	852	853	854	855	855	856
46	$\bar{1}$·857	858	858	859	860	861	861	862	863	863
47	$\bar{1}$·864	865	866	866	867	868	868	869	870	870
48	$\bar{1}$·871	872	872	873	874	874	875	876	876	877
49	$\bar{1}$·878	878	879	880	880	881	882	882	883	884
50	$\bar{1}$·884	885	886	886	887	887	888	888	889	890
51	$\bar{1}$·891	891	892	892	893	894	894	895	895	896
52	$\bar{1}$·897	897	898	898	899	899	900	901	901	902
53	$\bar{1}$·902	903	903	904	905	905	906	906	907	907
54	$\bar{1}$·908	909	909	910	910	911	911	912	912	913
55	$\bar{1}$·913	914	914	915	915	916	917	917	918	918
56	$\bar{1}$·919	919	920	920	921	921	922	922	923	923
57	$\bar{1}$·924	924	925	925	926	927	927	927	927	928
58	$\bar{1}$·928	929	929	930	930	931	931	932	932	933
59	$\bar{1}$·933	934	934	934	935	936	936	936	937	937
60	$\bar{1}$·938	938	938	939	939	940	940	941	941	941
61	$\bar{1}$·942	942	943	943	943	944	944	945	945	946
62	$\bar{1}$·946	946	947	947	948	948	948	949	949	949
63	$\bar{1}$·950	950	951	951	951	952	952	953	953	953
64	$\bar{1}$·954	954	954	955	955	955	956	956	957	957
65	$\bar{1}$·957	958	958	958	959	959	959	960	960	960
66	$\bar{1}$·961	961	961	962	962	962	963	963	963	964
67	$\bar{1}$·964	964	965	965	965	966	966	966	967	967
68	$\bar{1}$·967	967	968	968	968	969	969	969	970	970
69	$\bar{1}$·970	970	971	971	971	972	972	972	972	973
70	$\bar{1}$·973	973	974	974	974	974	975	975	975	975
71	$\bar{1}$·976	976	976	976	977	977	977	977	978	978
72	$\bar{1}$·978	978	979	979	979	979	980	980	980	980
73	$\bar{1}$·981	981	981	981	982	982	982	982	982	983
74	$\bar{1}$·983	983	983	983	984	984	984	984	985	985
75	$\bar{1}$·985	985	985	986	986	986	986	986	987	987
76	$\bar{1}$·987	987	987	987	988	988	988	988	988	989
77	$\bar{1}$·989	989	989	989	989	990	990	990	990	990
78	$\bar{1}$·990	990	991	991	991	991	991	991	992	992
79	$\bar{1}$·992	992	992	992	993	993	993	993	993	993
80	$\bar{1}$·993	993	994	994	994	994	994	994	994	994
81	$\bar{1}$·995	995	995	995	995	995	995	995	996	996
82	$\bar{1}$·996	996	996	996	996	996	996	996	997	997
83	$\bar{1}$·997	997	997	997	997	997	997	997	997	998
84	$\bar{1}$·998	998	998	998	998	998	998	998	998	998
85	$\bar{1}$·998	998	998	999	999	999	999	999	999	999
86	$\bar{1}$·999	999	999	999	999	999	999	999	999	999
87	$\bar{1}$·999	999	999	**000**	**000**	**000**	**000**	**000**	**000**	**000**
88	0·000	000	000	000	000	000	000	000	000	000
89	0·000	000	000	000	000	000	000	000	000	000

The **bold** type indicates that the integer changes.

LOGARITHMS OF COSINES

	0.0° 0′	0.1° 6′	0.2° 12′	0.3° 18′	0.4° 24′	0.5° 30′	0.6° 36′	0.7° 42′	0.8° 48′	0.9° 54′
0°	0·000	000	000	000	000	000	000	000	000	000
1	0·000	000	000	000	000	000	000	000	000	000
2	0·000	000	000	000	000	000	000	000	**999**	**999**
3	1̄·999	999	999	999	999	999	999	999	999	999
4	1̄·999	999	999	999	999	999	999	999	999	998
5	1̄·998	998	998	998	998	998	998	998	998	998
6	1̄·998	998	997	997	997	997	997	997	997	997
7	1̄·997	997	997	996	996	996	996	996	996	996
8	1̄·996	996	996	995	995	995	995	995	995	995
9	1̄·995	994	994	994	994	994	994	994	994	993
10	1̄·993	993	993	993	993	993	993	992	992	992
11	1̄·992	992	992	991	991	991	991	991	991	991
12	1̄·990	990	990	990	990	990	989	989	989	989
13	1̄·989	989	988	988	988	988	988	987	987	987
14	1̄·987	987	987	986	986	986	986	986	985	985
15	1̄·985	985	985	984	984	984	984	983	983	983
16	1̄·983	983	982	982	982	982	982	981	981	981
17	1̄·981	980	980	980	980	979	979	979	979	978
18	1̄·978	978	978	977	977	977	977	976	976	976
19	1̄·976	975	975	975	975	974	974	974	974	973
20	1̄·973	973	972	972	972	972	971	971	971	970
21	1̄·970	970	970	969	969	969	968	968	968	967
22	1̄·967	967	967	966	966	966	965	965	965	964
23	1̄·964	964	963	963	963	962	962	962	961	961
24	1̄·961	960	960	960	959	959	959	958	958	958
25	1̄·957	957	957	956	956	955	955	955	954	954
26	1̄·954	953	953	953	952	952	951	951	951	950
27	1̄·950	949	949	949	948	948	948	947	947	946
28	1̄·946	946	945	945	944	944	943	943	943	942
29	1̄·942	941	941	941	940	940	939	939	938	938
30	1̄·938	937	937	936	936	935	935	934	934	934
31	1̄·933	933	932	932	931	931	930	930	929	929
32	1̄·928	928	927	927	927	926	926	925	925	924
33	1̄·924	923	923	922	922	921	921	920	920	919
34	1̄·919	918	918	917	917	916	915	915	914	914
35	1̄·913	913	912	912	912	911	910	910	909	909
36	1̄·908	907	907	906	906	905	905	904	903	903
37	1̄·902	902	901	901	900	899	899	898	898	897
38	1̄·897	896	895	895	894	894	893	892	892	891
39	1̄·891	890	889	889	888	887	887	886	886	885
40	1̄·884	884	883	882	882	881	880	880	879	878
41	1̄·878	877	876	876	875	874	874	873	872	872
42	1̄·871	870	870	869	868	868	867	866	866	865
43	1̄·864	863	863	862	861	861	860	859	858	858
44	1̄·857	856	855	855	854	853	852	852	851	850

The **bold** type indicates that the integer changes.

LOGARITHMS OF COSINES

	0.0° 0′	0.1° 6′	0.2° 12′	0.3° 18′	0.4° 24′	0.5° 30′	0.6° 36′	0.7° 42′	0.8° 48′	0.9° 54′
45°	$\bar{1}$·849	849	848	847	846	846	845	844	843	843
46	$\bar{1}$·842	841	840	839	839	838	837	836	835	835
47	$\bar{1}$·834	833	832	831	831	830	829	828	827	826
48	$\bar{1}$·826	825	824	823	822	821	820	820	819	818
49	$\bar{1}$·817	816	815	814	813	813	812	811	810	809
50	$\bar{1}$·808	807	806	805	804	804	803	802	801	800
51	$\bar{1}$·799	798	797	796	795	794	793	792	791	790
52	$\bar{1}$·789	788	787	786	785	784	783	782	781	780
53	$\bar{1}$·779	778	777	776	775	774	773	772	771	770
54	$\bar{1}$·769	768	767	766	765	764	763	762	761	760
55	$\bar{1}$·759	758	756	755	754	753	752	751	750	749
56	$\bar{1}$·748	746	745	744	743	742	741	740	738	737
57	$\bar{1}$·736	735	734	733	731	730	729	728	727	725
58	$\bar{1}$·724	723	722	721	719	718	717	716	714	713
59	$\bar{1}$·712	711	709	708	707	705	704	703	702	700
60	$\bar{1}$·699	698	696	695	694	692	691	690	688	687
61	$\bar{1}$·686	684	683	681	680	679	677	676	674	673
62	$\bar{1}$·672	670	669	667	666	664	663	661	660	658
63	$\bar{1}$·657	656	654	653	651	650	648	646	645	643
64	$\bar{1}$·642	640	639	637	636	634	632	631	629	628
65	$\bar{1}$·626	624	623	621	619	618	616	614	613	611
66	$\bar{1}$·609	608	606	604	602	601	599	597	595	594
67	$\bar{1}$·592	590	588	586	585	583	581	579	577	575
68	$\bar{1}$·574	572	570	568	566	564	562	560	558	556
69	$\bar{1}$·554	552	550	548	546	544	542	540	538	536
70	$\bar{1}$·534	532	530	528	526	523	521	519	517	515
71	$\bar{1}$·513	510	508	506	504	501	499	497	495	492
72	$\bar{1}$·490	488	485	483	481	478	476	473	471	468
73	$\bar{1}$·466	463	461	458	456	453	451	448	446	443
74	$\bar{1}$·440	438	435	432	430	427	424	421	419	416
75	$\bar{1}$·413	410	407	404	402	399	396	393	390	387
76	$\bar{1}$·384	381	378	374	371	368	365	362	359	355
77	$\bar{1}$·352	349	345	342	339	335	332	328	325	321
78	$\bar{1}$·318	314	311	307	303	300	296	292	288	284
79	$\bar{1}$·281	277	273	269	265	261	257	252	248	244
80	$\bar{1}$·240	235	231	227	222	218	213	208	204	199
81	$\bar{1}$·194	189	190	180	175	170	165	159	154	149
82	$\bar{1}$·144	138	133	127	121	116	110	104	098	092
83	$\bar{1}$·086	080	073	067	060	054	047	040	033	026
84	$\bar{1}$·019	012	005	**997**	**989**	**982**	**974**	**966**	**957**	**949**
85	$\bar{2}$·940	932	923	913	904	895	885	875	865	854
86	$\bar{2}$·844	833	821	810	798	786	773	760	747	733
87	$\bar{2}$·719	704	689	673	657	640	622	603	584	564
88	$\bar{2}$·543	521	497	472	446	418	388	356	321	283
89	$\bar{2}$·242	196	145	087	020	**$\bar{3}$·941**	844	719	543	242

The **bold** type indicates that the integer changes.

LOGARITHMS OF TANGENTS

	0.0° 0′	0.1° 6′	0.2° 12′	0.3° 18′	0.4° 24′	0.5° 30′	0.6° 36′	0.7° 42′	0.8° 48′	0.9° 54′
0°	−∞	$\bar{3}$·242	$\bar{3}$·543	$\bar{3}$·719	$\bar{3}$·844	$\bar{3}$·941	$\bar{2}$·020	$\bar{2}$·087	$\bar{2}$·145	$\bar{2}$·196
1	$\bar{2}$·242	283	321	356	388	418	446	472	497	521
2	$\bar{2}$·543	564	585	604	622	640	657	674	689	705
3	$\bar{2}$·719	734	747	761	774	786	799	811	822	834
4	$\bar{2}$·845	855	866	876	886	896	906	915	924	933
5	$\bar{2}$·942	951	959	967	976	984	991	999	**007**	**014**
6	$\bar{1}$·022	029	036	043	050	057	063	070	076	083
7	$\bar{1}$·089	095	102	108	114	119	125	131	137	142
8	$\bar{1}$·148	153	159	164	169	174	180	185	190	195
9	$\bar{1}$·200	205	209	214	219	224	228	233	237	242
10	$\bar{1}$·246	251	255	259	264	268	272	276	280	285
11	$\bar{1}$·289	293	297	301	305	308	312	316	320	324
12	$\bar{1}$·327	331	335	339	342	346	349	353	356	360
13	$\bar{1}$·363	367	370	374	377	380	384	387	390	394
14	$\bar{1}$·397	400	403	406	410	413	416	419	422	425
15	$\bar{1}$·428	431	434	437	440	443	446	449	452	455
16	$\bar{1}$·457	460	463	466	469	472	474	477	480	483
17	$\bar{1}$·485	488	491	493	496	499	501	504	507	509
18	$\bar{1}$·512	514	517	519	522	525	527	530	532	535
19	$\bar{1}$·537	539	542	544	547	549	552	554	556	559
20	$\bar{1}$·561	563	566	568	570	573	575	577	580	582
21	$\bar{1}$·584	586	589	591	593	595	598	600	602	604
22	$\bar{1}$·606	609	611	613	615	617	619	621	624	626
23	$\bar{1}$·628	630	632	634	636	638	640	642	644	647
24	$\bar{1}$·649	651	653	655	657	659	661	663	665	667
25	$\bar{1}$·669	671	673	675	677	678	680	682	684	686
26	$\bar{1}$·688	690	692	694	696	698	700	702	703	705
27	$\bar{1}$·707	709	711	713	715	716	718	720	722	724
28	$\bar{1}$·726	728	729	731	733	735	737	738	740	742
29	$\bar{1}$·744	746	747	749	751	753	754	756	758	760
30	$\bar{1}$·761	763	765	767	768	770	772	774	775	777
31	$\bar{1}$·779	780	782	784	786	787	789	791	792	794
32	$\bar{1}$·796	797	799	801	803	804	806	808	809	811
33	$\bar{1}$·813	814	816	817	819	821	822	824	826	827
34	$\bar{1}$·829	831	832	834	836	837	839	840	842	844
35	$\bar{1}$·845	847	848	850	852	853	855	856	858	860
36	$\bar{1}$·861	863	864	866	868	869	871	872	874	876
37	$\bar{1}$·877	879	880	882	883	885	887	888	890	891
38	$\bar{1}$·893	894	896	897	899	901	902	904	905	907
39	$\bar{1}$·908	910	911	913	915	916	918	919	921	922
40	$\bar{1}$·924	925	927	928	930	931	933	935	936	938
41	$\bar{1}$·939	941	942	944	945	947	948	950	951	953
42	$\bar{1}$·954	956	957	959	961	962	964	965	967	968
43	$\bar{1}$·970	971	973	974	976	977	979	980	982	983
44	$\bar{1}$·985	986	988	989	991	992	994	995	997	998

The **bold** type indicates that the integer changes.

LOGARITHMS OF TANGENTS

	0.0° 0′	0.1° 6′	0.2° 12′	0.3° 18′	0.4° 24′	0.5° 30′	0.6° 36′	0.7° 42′	0.8° 48′	0.9° 54′
45°	0·000	002	003	005	006	008	009	011	012	014
46	0·015	017	018	020	021	023	024	026	027	029
47	0·030	032	033	035	036	038	039	041	043	044
48	0·046	047	049	050	052	053	055	056	058	059
49	0·061	062	064	065	067	069	070	072	073	075
50	0·076	078	079	081	082	084	085	087	089	090
51	0·092	093	095	096	098	099	101	103	104	106
52	0·107	109	110	112	113	115	117	118	120	121
53	0·123	124	126	128	129	131	132	134	136	137
54	0·139	140	142	144	145	147	148	150	152	153
55	0·155	156	158	160	161	163	164	166	168	169
56	0·171	173	174	176	178	179	181	183	184	186
57	0·187	189	191	192	194	196	197	199	201	203
58	0·204	206	208	209	211	213	214	216	218	220
59	0·221	223	225	226	228	230	232	233	235	237
60	0·239	240	242	244	246	247	249	251	253	254
61	0·256	258	260	262	263	265	267	269	271	272
62	0·274	276	278	280	282	284	285	287	289	291
63	0·293	295	297	298	300	302	304	306	308	310
64	0·312	314	316	318	320	322	323	325	327	329
65	0·331	333	335	337	339	341	343	345	347	349
66	0·351	353	356	358	360	362	364	366	368	370
67	0·372	374	376	379	381	383	385	387	389	391
68	0·394	396	398	400	402	405	407	409	411	414
69	0·416	418	420	423	425	427	430	432	434	437
70	0·439	441	444	446	448	451	453	456	458	461
71	0·463	465	468	470	473	475	478	481	483	486
72	0·488	491	493	496	499	501	504	507	509	512
73	0·515	517	520	523	526	528	531	534	537	540
74	0·543	545	548	551	554	557	560	563	566	569
75	0·572	575	578	581	584	587	590	594	597	600
76	0·603	606	610	613	616	620	623	626	630	633
77	0·637	640	644	647	651	654	658	661	665	669
78	0·673	676	680	684	688	692	695	699	703	707
79	0·711	715	720	724	728	732	736	741	745	749
80	0·754	758	763	767	772	776	781	786	791	795
81	0·800	805	810	815	820	826	831	836	841	847
82	0·852	858	863	869	875	881	886	892	898	905
83	0·911	917	924	930	937	943	950	957	964	971
84	0·978	986	993	**001**	**009**	**016**	**024**	**033**	**041**	**049**
85	1·058	067	076	085	094	104	114	124	134	145
86	1·155	166	178	189	201	214	226	239	253	266
87	1·281	295	311	326	343	360	378	396	415	436
88	1·457	479	503	528	554	582	612	644	679	717
89	1·758	1·804	1·855	1·913	1·980	2·059	2·156	2·281	2·457	2·758

The **bold** type indicates that the integer changes.

SQUARES

	0	1	2	3	4	5	6	7	8	9
1·0	1·00	1·02	1·04	1·06	1·08	1·10	1·12	1·14	1·17	1·19
1·1	1·21	1·23	1·25	1·28	1·30	1·32	1·35	1·37	1·39	1·42
1·2	1·44	1·46	1·49	1·51	1·54	1·56	1·59	1·61	1·64	1·66
1·3	1·69	1·72	1·74	1·77	1·80	1·82	1·85	1·88	1·90	1·93
1·4	1·96	1·99	2·02	2·04	2·07	2·10	2·13	2·16	2·19	2·22
1·5	2·25	2·28	2·31	2·34	2·37	2·40	2·43	2·46	2·50	2·53
1·6	2·56	2·59	2·62	2·66	2·69	2·72	2·76	2·79	2·82	2·86
1·7	2·89	2·92	2·96	2·99	3·03	3·06	3·10	3·13	3·17	3·20
1·8	3·24	3·28	3·31	3·35	3·39	3·42	3·46	3·50	3·53	3·57
1·9	3·61	3·65	3·69	3·72	3·76	3·80	3·84	3·88	3·92	3·96
2·0	4·00	4·04	4·08	4·12	4·16	4·20	4·24	4·28	4·33	4·37
2·1	4·41	4·45	4·49	4·54	4·58	4·62	4·67	4·71	4·75	4·80
2·2	4·84	4·88	4·93	4·97	5·02	5·06	5·11	5·15	5·20	5·24
2·3	5·29	5·34	5·38	5·43	5·48	5·52	5·57	5·62	5·66	5·71
2·4	5·76	5·81	5·86	5·90	5·95	6·00	6·05	6·10	6·15	6·20
2·5	6·25	6·30	6·35	6·40	6·45	6·50	6·55	6·60	6·66	6·71
2·6	6·76	6·81	6·86	6·92	6·97	7·02	7·08	7·13	7·18	7·24
2·7	7·29	7·34	7·40	7·45	7·51	7·56	7·62	7·67	7·73	7·78
2·8	7·84	7·90	7·95	8·01	8·07	8·12	8·18	8·24	8·29	8·35
2·9	8·41	8·47	8·53	8·58	8·64	8·70	8·76	8·82	8·88	8·94
3·0	9·00	9·06	9·12	9·18	9·24	9·30	9·36	9·42	9·49	9·55
3·1	9·61	9·67	9·73	9·80	9·86	9·92	9·99	10·0	10·1	10·2
3·2	10·2	10·3	10·4	10·4	10·5	10·6	10·6	10·7	10·8	10·8
3·3	10·9	11·0	11·0	11·1	11·2	11·2	11·3	11·4	11·4	11·5
3·4	11·6	11·6	11·7	11·8	11·8	11·9	12·0	12·0	12·1	12·2
3·5	12·3	12·3	12·4	12·5	12·5	12·6	12·7	12·7	12·8	12·9
3·6	13·0	13·0	13·1	13·2	13·2	13·3	13·4	13·5	13·5	13·6
3·7	13·7	13·8	13·8	13·9	14·0	14·1	14·1	14·2	14·3	14·4
3·8	14·4	14·5	14·6	14·7	14·7	14·8	14·9	15·0	15·1	15·1
3·9	15·2	15·3	15·4	15·4	15·5	15·6	15·7	15·8	15·8	15·9
4·0	16·0	16·1	16·2	16·2	16·3	16·4	16·5	16·6	16·6	16·7
4·1	16·8	16·9	17·0	17·1	17·1	17·2	17·3	17·4	17·5	17·6
4·2	17·6	17·7	17·8	17·9	18·0	18·1	18·1	18·2	18·3	18·4
4·3	18·5	18·6	18·7	18·7	18·8	18·9	19·0	19·1	19·2	19·3
4·4	19·4	19·4	19·5	19·6	19·7	19·8	19·9	20·0	20·1	20·2
4·5	20·3	20·3	20·4	20·5	20·6	20·7	20·8	20·9	21·0	21·1
4·6	21·2	21·3	21·3	21·4	21·5	21·6	21·7	21·8	21·9	22·0
4·7	22·1	22·2	22·3	22·4	22·5	22·6	22·7	22·8	22·8	22·9
4·8	23·0	23·1	23·2	23·3	23·4	23·5	23·6	23·7	23·8	23·9
4·9	24·0	24·1	24·2	24·3	24·4	24·5	24·6	24·7	24·8	24·9
5·0	25·0	25·1	25·2	25·3	25·4	25·5	25·6	25·7	25·8	25·9
5·1	26·0	26·1	26·2	26·3	26·4	26·5	26·6	26·7	26·8	26·9
5·2	27·0	27·1	27·2	27·4	27·5	27·6	27·7	27·8	27·9	28·0
5·3	28·1	28·2	28·3	28·4	28·5	28·6	28·7	28·8	28·9	29·1
5·4	29·2	29·3	29·4	29·5	29·6	29·7	29·8	29·9	30·0	30·1

SQUARES

	0	1	2	3	4	5	6	7	8	9
5·5	30·3	30·4	30·5	30·6	30·7	30·8	30·9	31·0	31·1	31·2
5·6	31·4	31·5	31·6	31·7	31·8	31·9	32·0	32·1	32·3	32·4
5·7	32·5	32·6	32·7	32·8	32·9	33·1	33·2	33·3	33·4	33·5
5·8	33·6	33·8	33·9	34·0	34·1	34·2	34·3	34·5	34·6	34·7
5·9	34·8	34·9	35·0	35·2	35·3	35·4	35·5	35·6	35·8	35·9
6·0	36·0	36·1	36·2	36·4	36·5	36·6	36·7	36·8	37·0	37·1
6·1	37·2	37·3	37·5	37·6	37·7	37·8	37·9	38·1	38·2	38·3
6·2	38·4	38·6	38·7	38·8	38·9	39·1	39·2	39·3	39·4	39·6
6·3	39·7	39·8	39·9	40·1	40·2	40·3	40·4	40·6	40·7	40·8
6·4	41·0	41·1	41·2	41·3	41·5	41·6	41·7	41·9	42·0	42·1
6·5	42·3	42·4	42·5	42·6	42·8	42·9	43·0	43·2	43·3	43·4
6·6	43·6	43·7	43·8	44·0	44·1	44·2	44·4	44·5	44·6	44·8
6·7	44·9	45·0	45·2	45·3	45·4	45·6	45·7	45·8	46·0	46·1
6·8	46·2	46·4	46·5	46·6	46·8	46·9	47·1	47·2	47·3	47·5
6·9	47·6	47·7	47·9	48·0	48·2	48·3	48·4	48·6	48·7	48·9
7·0	49·0	49·1	49·3	49·4	49·6	49·7	49·8	50·0	50·1	50·3
7·1	50·4	50·6	50·7	50·8	51·0	51·1	51·3	51·4	51·6	51·7
7·2	51·8	52·0	52·1	52·3	52·4	52·6	52·7	52·9	53·0	53·1
7·3	53·3	53·4	53·6	53·7	53·9	54·0	54·2	54·3	54·5	54·6
7·4	54·8	54·9	55·1	55·2	55·4	55·5	55·7	55·8	56·0	56·1
7·5	56·3	56·4	56·6	56·7	56·9	57·0	57·2	57·3	57·5	57·6
7·6	57·8	57·9	58·1	58·2	58·4	58·5	58·7	58·8	59·0	59·1
7·7	59·3	59·4	59·6	59·8	59·9	60·1	60·2	60·4	60·5	60·7
7·8	60·8	61·0	61·2	61·3	61·5	61·6	61·8	61·9	62·1	62·3
7·9	62·4	62·6	62·7	62·9	63·0	63·2	63·4	63·5	63·7	63·8
8·0	64·0	64·2	64·3	64·5	64·6	64·8	65·0	65·1	65·3	65·4
8·1	65·6	65·8	65·9	66·1	66·3	66·4	66·6	66·7	66·9	67·1
8·2	67·2	67·4	67·6	67·7	67·9	68·1	68·2	68·4	68·6	68·7
8·3	68·9	69·1	69·2	69·4	69·6	69·7	69·9	70·1	70·2	70·4
8·4	70·6	70·7	70·9	71·1	71·2	71·4	71·6	71·7	71·9	72·1
8·5	72·3	72·4	72·6	72·8	72·9	73·1	73·3	73·4	73·6	73·8
8·6	74·0	74·1	74·3	74·5	74·6	74·8	75·0	75·2	75·3	75·5
8·7	75·7	75·9	76·0	76·2	76·4	76·6	76·7	76·9	77·1	77·3
8·8	77·4	77·6	77·8	78·0	78·1	78·3	78·5	78·7	78·9	79·0
8·9	79·2	79·4	79·6	79·7	79·9	80·1	80·3	80·5	80·6	80·8
9·0	81·0	81·2	81·4	81·5	81·7	81·9	82·1	82·3	82·4	82·6
9·1	82·8	83·0	83·2	83·4	83·5	83·7	83·9	84·1	84·3	84·5
9·2	84·6	84·8	85·0	85·2	85·4	85·6	85·7	85·9	86·1	86·3
9·3	86·5	86·7	86·9	87·0	87·2	87·4	87·6	87·8	88·0	88·2
9·4	88·4	88·5	88·7	88·9	89·1	89·3	89·5	89·7	89·9	90·1
9·5	90·3	90·4	90·6	90·8	91·0	91·2	91·4	91·6	91·8	92·0
9·6	92·2	92·4	92·5	92·7	92·9	93·1	93·3	93·5	93·7	93·9
9·7	94·1	94·3	94·5	94·7	94·9	95·1	95·3	95·5	95·6	95·8
9·8	96·0	96·2	96·4	96·6	96·8	97·0	97·2	97·4	97·6	97·8
9·9	98·0	98·2	98·4	98·6	98·8	99·0	99·2	99·4	99·6	99·8
10·0	100									

SQUARE ROOTS OF NUMBERS FROM 1 TO 10

	0	1	2	3	4	5	6	7	8	9
1·0	1·00	1·00	1·01	1·01	1·02	1·02	1·03	1·03	1·04	1·04
1·1	1·05	1·05	1·06	1·06	1·07	1·07	1·08	1·08	1·09	1·09
1·2	1·10	1·10	1·10	1·11	1·11	1·12	1·12	1·13	1·13	1·14
1·3	1·14	1·14	1·15	1·15	1·16	1·16	1·17	1·17	1·17	1·18
1·4	1·18	1·19	1·19	1·20	1·20	1·20	1·21	1·21	1·22	1·22
1·5	1·22	1·23	1·23	1·24	1·24	1·24	1·25	1·25	1·26	1·26
1·6	1·26	1·27	1·27	1·28	1·28	1·28	1·29	1·29	1·30	1·30
1·7	1·30	1·31	1·31	1·32	1·32	1·32	1·33	1·33	1·33	1·34
1·8	1·34	1·35	1·35	1·35	1·36	1·36	1·36	1·37	1·37	1·37
1·9	1·38	1·38	1·39	1·39	1·39	1·40	1·40	1·40	1·41	1·41
2·0	1·41	1·42	1·42	1·42	1·43	1·43	1·44	1·44	1·44	1·45
2·1	1·45	1·45	1·46	1·46	1·46	1·47	1·47	1·47	1·48	1·48
2·2	1·48	1·49	1·49	1·49	1·50	1·50	1·50	1·51	1·51	1·51
2·3	1·52	1·52	1·52	1·53	1·53	1·53	1·54	1·54	1·54	1·55
2·4	1·55	1·55	1·56	1·56	1·56	1·57	1·57	1·57	1·57	1·58
2·5	1·58	1·58	1·59	1·59	1·59	1·60	1·60	1·60	1·61	1·61
2·6	1·61	1·62	1·62	1·62	1·62	1·63	1·63	1·63	1·64	1·64
2·7	1·64	1·65	1·65	1·65	1·66	1·66	1·66	1·66	1·67	1·67
2·8	1·67	1·68	1·68	1·68	1·69	1·69	1·69	1·69	1·70	1·70
2·9	1·70	1·71	1·71	1·71	1·71	1·72	1·72	1·72	1·73	1·73
3·0	1·73	1·73	1·74	1·74	1·74	1·75	1·75	1·75	1·75	1·76
3·1	1·76	1·76	1·77	1·77	1·77	1·77	1·78	1·78	1·78	1·79
3·2	1·79	1·79	1·79	1·80	1·80	1·80	1·81	1·81	1·81	1·81
3·3	1·82	1·82	1·82	1·82	1·83	1·83	1·83	1·84	1·84	1·84
3·4	1·84	1·85	1·85	1·85	1·85	1·86	1·86	1·86	1·87	1·87
3·5	1·87	1·87	1·88	1·88	1·88	1·88	1·89	1·89	1·89	1·89
3·6	1·90	1·90	1·90	1·91	1·91	1·91	1·91	1·92	1·92	1·92
3·7	1·92	1·93	1·93	1·93	1·93	1·94	1·94	1·94	1·94	1·95
3·8	1·95	1·95	1·95	1·96	1·96	1·96	1·96	1·97	1·97	1·97
3·9	1·97	1·98	1·98	1·98	1·98	1·99	1·99	1·99	1·99	2·00
4·0	2·00	2·00	2·00	2·01	2·01	2·01	2·01	2·02	2·02	2·02
4·1	2·02	2·03	2·03	2·03	2·03	2·04	2·04	2·04	2·04	2·05
4·2	2·05	2·05	2·05	2·06	2·06	2·06	2·06	2·07	2·07	2·07
4·3	2·07	2·08	2·08	2·08	2·08	2·09	2·09	2·09	2·09	2·10
4·4	2·10	2·10	2·10	2·10	2·11	2·11	2·11	2·11	2·12	2·12
4·5	2·12	2·12	2·13	2·13	2·13	2·13	2·14	2·14	2·14	2·14
4·6	2·14	2·15	2·15	2·15	2·15	2·16	2·16	2·16	2·16	2·17
4·7	2·17	2·17	2·17	2·17	2·18	2·18	2·18	2·18	2·19	2·19
4·8	2·19	2·19	2·20	2·20	2·20	2·20	2·20	2·21	2·21	2·21
4·9	2·21	2·22	2·22	2·22	2·22	2·22	2·23	2·23	2·23	2·23
5·0	2·24	2·24	2·24	2·24	2·24	2·25	2·25	2·25	2·25	2·26
5·1	2·26	2·26	2·26	2·26	2·27	2·27	2·27	2·27	2·28	2·28
5·2	2·28	2·28	2·28	2·29	2·29	2·29	2·29	2·30	2·30	2·30
5·3	2·30	2·30	2·31	2·31	2·31	2·31	2·32	2·32	2·32	2·32
5·4	2·32	2·33	2·33	2·33	2·33	2·33	2·34	2·34	2·34	2·34

SQUARE ROOTS OF NUMBERS FROM 1 TO 10

	0	1	2	3	4	5	6	7	8	9
5·5	2·35	2·35	2·35	2·35	2·35	2·36	2·36	2·36	2·36	2·36
5·6	2·37	2·37	2·37	2·37	2·37	2·38	2·38	2·38	2·38	2·39
5·7	2·39	2·39	2·39	2·39	2·40	2·40	2·40	2·40	2·40	2·41
5·8	2·41	2·41	2·41	2·41	2·42	2·42	2·42	2·42	2·42	2·43
5·9	2·43	2·43	2·43	2·44	2·44	2·44	2·44	2·44	2·45	2·45
6·0	2·45	2·45	2·45	2·46	2·46	2·46	2·46	2·46	2·47	2·47
6·1	2·47	2·47	2·47	2·48	2·48	2·48	2·48	2·48	2·49	2·49
6·2	2·49	2·49	2·49	2·50	2·50	2·50	2·50	2·50	2·51	2·51
6·3	2·51	2·51	2·51	2·52	2·52	2·52	2·52	2·52	2·53	2·53
6·4	2·53	2·53	2·53	2·54	2·54	2·54	2·54	2·54	2·55	2·55
6·5	2·55	2·55	2·55	2·56	2·56	2·56	2·56	2·56	2·57	2·57
6·6	2·57	2·57	2·57	2·57	2·58	2·58	2·58	2·58	2·58	2·59
6·7	2·59	2·59	2·59	2·59	2·60	2·60	2·60	2·60	2·60	2·61
6·8	2·61	2·61	2·61	2·61	2·62	2·62	2·62	2·62	2·62	2·62
6·9	2·63	2·63	2·63	2·63	2·63	2·64	2·64	2·64	2·64	2·64
7·0	2·65	2·65	2·65	2·65	2·65	2·66	2·66	2·66	2·66	2·66
7·1	2·66	2·67	2·67	2·67	2·67	2·67	2·68	2·68	2·68	2·68
7·2	2·68	2·69	2·69	2·69	2·69	2·69	2·69	2·70	2·70	2·70
7·3	2·70	2·70	2·71	2·71	2·71	2·71	2·71	2·71	2·72	2·72
7·4	2·72	2·72	2·72	2·73	2·73	2·73	2·73	2·73	2·73	2·74
7·5	2·74	2·74	2·74	2·74	2·75	2·75	2·75	2·75	2·75	2·75
7·6	2·76	2·76	2·76	2·76	2·76	2·77	2·77	2·77	2·77	2·77
7·7	2·77	2·78	2·78	2·78	2·78	2·78	2·79	2·79	2·79	2·79
7·8	2·79	2·79	2·80	2·80	2·80	2·80	2·80	2·81	2·81	2·81
7·9	2·81	2·81	2·81	2·82	2·82	2·82	2·82	2·82	2·82	2·83
8·0	2·83	2·83	2·83	2·83	2·84	2·84	2·84	2·84	2·84	2·84
8·1	2·85	2·85	2·85	2·85	2·85	2·85	2·86	2·86	2·86	2·86
8·2	2·86	2·87	2·87	2·87	2·87	2·87	2·87	2·88	2·88	2·88
8·3	2·88	2·88	2·88	2·89	2·89	2·89	2·89	2·89	2·89	2·90
8·4	2·90	2·90	2·90	2·90	2·91	2·91	2·91	2·91	2·91	2·91
8·5	2·92	2·92	2·92	2·92	2·92	2·92	2·93	2·93	2·93	2·93
8·6	2·93	2·93	2·94	2·94	2·94	2·94	2·94	2·94	2·95	2·95
8·7	2·95	2·95	2·95	2·95	2·96	2·96	2·96	2·96	2·96	2·96
8·8	2·97	2·97	2·97	2·97	2·97	2·97	2·98	2·98	2·98	2·98
8·9	2·98	2·98	2·99	2·99	2·99	2·99	2·99	2·99	3·00	3·00
9·0	3·00	3·00	3·00	3·00	3·01	3·01	3·01	3·01	3·01	3·01
9·1	3·02	3·02	3·02	3·02	3·02	3·02	3·03	3·03	3·03	3·03
9·2	3·03	3·03	3·04	3·04	3·04	3·04	3·04	3·04	3·05	3·05
9·3	3·05	3·05	3·05	3·05	3·06	3·06	3·06	3·06	3·06	3·06
9·4	3·07	3·07	3·07	3·07	3·07	3·07	3·08	3·08	3·08	3·08
9·5	3·08	3·08	3·09	3·09	3·09	3·09	3·09	3·09	3·10	3·10
9·6	3·10	3·10	3·10	3·10	3·10	3·11	3·11	3·11	3·11	3·11
9·7	3·11	3·12	3·12	3·12	3·12	3·12	3·12	3·13	3·13	3·13
9·8	3·13	3·13	3·13	3·14	3·14	3·14	3·14	3·14	3·14	3·14
9·9	3·15	3·15	3·15	3·15	3·15	3·15	3·16	3·16	3·16	3·16
10·0	3·16									

SQUARE ROOTS OF NUMBERS FROM 10 TO 99

	0	1	2	3	4	5	6	7	8	9
10	3·16	3·18	3·19	3·21	3·22	3·24	3·26	3·27	3·29	3·30
11	3·32	3·33	3·35	3·36	3·38	3·39	3·41	3·42	3·44	3·45
12	3·46	3·48	3·49	3·51	3·52	3·54	3·55	3·56	3·58	3·59
13	3·61	3·62	3·63	3·65	3·66	3·67	3·69	3·70	3·71	3·73
14	3·74	3·75	3·77	3·78	3·79	3·81	3·82	3·83	3·85	3·86
15	3·87	3·89	3·90	3·91	3·92	3·94	3·95	3·96	3·97	3·99
16	4·00	4·01	4·02	4·04	4·05	4·06	4·07	4·09	4·10	4·11
17	4·12	4·14	4·15	4·16	4·17	4·18	4·20	4·21	4·22	4·23
18	4·24	4·25	4·27	4·28	4·29	4·30	4·31	4·32	4·34	4·35
19	4·36	4·37	4·38	4·39	4·40	4·42	4·43	4·44	4·45	4·46
20	4·47	4·48	4·49	4·51	4·52	4·53	4·54	4·55	4·56	4·57
21	4·58	4·59	4·60	4·62	4·63	4·64	4·65	4·66	4·67	4·68
22	4·69	4·70	4·71	4·72	4·73	4·74	4·75	4·76	4·77	4·79
23	4·80	4·81	4·82	4·83	4·84	4·85	4·86	4·87	4·88	4·89
24	4·90	4·91	4·92	4·93	4·94	4·95	4·96	4·97	4·98	4·99
25	5·00	5·01	5·02	5·03	5·04	5·05	5·06	5·07	5·08	5·09
26	5·10	5·11	5·12	5·13	5·14	5·15	5·16	5·17	5·18	5·19
27	5·20	5·21	5·22	5·22	5·23	5·24	5·25	5·26	5·27	5·28
28	5·29	5·30	5·31	5·32	5·33	5·34	5·35	5·36	5·37	5·38
29	5·39	5·39	5·40	5·41	5·42	5·43	5·44	5·45	5·46	5·47
30	5·48	5·49	5·50	5·50	5·51	5·52	5·53	5·54	5·55	5·56
31	5·57	5·58	5·59	5·59	5·60	5·61	5·62	5·63	5·64	5·65
32	5·66	5·67	5·67	5·68	5·69	5·70	5·71	5·72	5·73	5·74
33	5·74	5·75	5·76	5·77	5·78	5·79	5·80	5·81	5·81	5·82
34	5·83	5·84	5·85	5·86	5·87	5·87	5·88	5·89	5·90	5·91
35	5·92	5·92	5·93	5·94	5·95	5·96	5·97	5·97	5·98	5·99
36	6·00	6·01	6·02	6·02	6·03	6·04	6·05	6·06	6·07	6·07
37	6·08	6·09	6·10	6·11	6·12	6·12	6·13	6·14	6·15	6·16
38	6·16	6·17	6·18	6·19	6·20	6·20	6·21	6·22	6·23	6·24
39	6·24	6·25	6·26	6·27	6·28	6·28	6·29	6·30	6·31	6·32
40	6·32	6·33	6·34	6·35	6·36	6·36	6·37	6·38	6·39	6·40
41	6·40	6·41	6·42	6·43	6·43	6·44	6·45	6·46	6·47	6·47
42	6·48	6·49	6·50	6·50	6·51	6·52	6·53	6·53	6·54	6·55
43	6·56	6·57	6·57	6·58	6·59	6·60	6·60	6·61	6·62	6·63
44	6·63	6·64	6·65	6·66	6·66	6·67	6·68	6·69	6·69	6·70
45	6·71	6·72	6·72	6·73	6·74	6·75	6·75	6·76	6·77	6·77
46	6·78	6·79	6·80	6·80	6·81	6·82	6·83	6·83	6·84	6·85
47	6·86	6·86	6·87	6·88	6·88	6·89	6·90	6·91	6·91	6·92
48	6·93	6·94	6·94	6·95	6·96	6·96	6·97	6·98	6·99	6·99
49	7·00	7·01	7·01	7·02	7·03	7·04	7·04	7·05	7·06	7·06
50	7·07	7·08	7·09	7·09	7·10	7·11	7·11	7·12	7·13	7·13
51	7·14	7·15	7·16	7·16	7·17	7·18	7·18	7·19	7·20	7·20
52	7·21	7·22	7·22	7·23	7·24	7·25	7·25	7·26	7·27	7·27
53	7·28	7·29	7·29	7·30	7·31	7·31	7·32	7·33	7·33	7·34
54	7·35	7·36	7·36	7·37	7·38	7·38	7·39	7·40	7·40	7·41

SQUARE ROOTS OF NUMBERS FROM 10 TO 99

	0	1	2	3	4	5	6	7	8	9
55	7·42	7·42	7·43	7·44	7·44	7·45	7·46	7·46	7·47	7·48
56	7·48	7·49	7·50	7·50	7·51	7·52	7·52	7·53	7·54	7·54
57	7·55	7·56	7·56	7·57	7·58	7·58	7·59	7·60	7·60	7·61
58	7·62	7·62	7·63	7·64	7·64	7·65	7·66	7·66	7·67	7·67
59	7·68	7·69	7·69	7·70	7·71	7·71	7·72	7·73	7·73	7·74
60	7·75	7·75	7·76	7·77	7·77	7·78	7·78	7·79	7·80	7·80
61	7·81	7·82	7·82	7·83	7·84	7·84	7·85	7·85	7·86	7·87
62	7·87	7·88	7·89	7·89	7·90	7·91	7·91	7·92	7·92	7·93
63	7·94	7·94	7·95	7·96	7·96	7·97	7·97	7·98	7·99	7·99
64	8·00	8·01	8·01	8·02	8·02	8·03	8·04	8·04	8·05	8·06
65	8·06	8·07	8·07	8·08	8·09	8·09	8·10	8·11	8·11	8·12
66	8·12	8·13	8·14	8·14	8·15	8·15	8·16	8·17	8·17	8·18
67	8·19	8·19	8·20	8·20	8·21	8·22	8·22	8·23	8·23	8·24
68	8·25	8·25	8·26	8·26	8·27	8·28	8·28	8·29	8·29	8·30
69	8·31	8·31	8·32	8·32	8·33	8·34	8·34	8·35	8·35	8·36
70	8·37	8·37	8·38	8·38	8·39	8·40	8·40	8·41	8·41	8·42
71	8·43	8·43	8·44	8·44	8·45	8·46	8·46	8·47	8·47	8·48
72	8·49	8·49	8·50	8·50	8·51	8·51	8·52	8·53	8·53	8·54
73	8·54	8·55	8·56	8·56	8·57	8·57	8·58	8·58	8·59	8·60
74	8·60	8·61	8·61	8·62	8·63	8·63	8·64	8·64	8·65	8·65
75	8·66	8·67	8·67	8·68	8·68	8·69	8·69	8·70	8·71	8·71
76	8·72	8·72	8·73	8·73	8·74	8·75	8·75	8·76	8·76	8·77
77	8·77	8·78	8·79	8·79	8·80	8·80	8·81	8·81	8·82	8·83
78	8·83	8·84	8·84	8·85	8·85	8·86	8·87	8·87	8·88	8·88
79	8·89	8·89	8·90	8·91	8·91	8·92	8·92	8·93	8·93	8·94
80	8·94	8·95	8·96	8·96	8·97	8·97	8·98	8·98	8·99	8·99
81	9·00	9·01	9·01	9·02	9·02	9·03	9·03	9·04	9·04	9·05
82	9·06	9·06	9·07	9·07	9·08	9·08	9·09	9·09	9·10	9·10
83	9·11	9·12	9·12	9·13	9·13	9·14	9·14	9·15	9·15	9·16
84	9·17	9·17	9·18	9·18	9·19	9·19	9·20	9·20	9·21	9·21
85	9·22	9·22	9·23	9·24	9·24	9·25	9·25	9·26	9·26	9·27
86	9·27	9·28	9·28	9·29	9·30	9·30	9·31	9·31	9·32	9·32
87	9·33	9·33	9·34	9·34	9·35	9·35	9·36	9·36	9·37	9·38
88	9·38	9·39	9·39	9·40	9·40	9·41	9·41	9·42	9·42	9·43
89	9·43	9·44	9·44	9·45	9·46	9·46	9·47	9·47	9·48	9·48
90	9·49	9·49	9·50	9·50	9·51	9·51	9·52	9·52	9·53	9·53
91	9·54	9·54	9·55	9·56	9·56	9·57	9·57	9·58	9·58	9·59
92	9·59	9·60	9·60	9·61	9·61	9·62	9·62	9·63	9·63	9·64
93	9·64	9·65	9·65	9·66	9·66	9·67	9·67	9·68	9·69	9·69
94	9·70	9·70	9·71	9·71	9·72	9·72	9·73	9·73	9·74	9·74
95	9·75	9·75	9·76	9·76	9·77	9·77	9·78	9·78	9·79	9·79
96	9·80	9·80	9·81	9·81	9·82	9·82	9·83	9·83	9·84	9·84
97	9·85	9·85	9·86	9·86	9·87	9·87	9·88	9·88	9·89	9·89
98	9·90	9·90	9·91	9·91	9·92	9·92	9·93	9·93	9·94	9·94
99	9·95	9·95	9·96	9·96	9·97	9·97	9·98	9·98	9·99	9·99

RECIPROCALS

	0	1	2	3	4	5	6	7	8	9
1·0	1·00	·990	·980	·971	·962	·952	·943	·935	·926	·917
1·1	0·909	·901	·893	·885	·877	·870	·862	·855	·847	·840
1·2	0·833	·826	·820	·813	·806	·800	·794	·787	·781	·775
1·3	0·769	·763	·758	·752	·746	·741	·735	·730	·725	·719
1·4	0·714	·709	·704	·699	·694	·690	·685	·680	·676	·671
1·5	0·667	·662	·658	·654	·649	·645	·641	·637	·633	·629
1·6	0·625	·621	·617	·613	·610	·606	·602	·599	·595	·592
1·7	0·588	·585	·581	·578	·575	·571	·568	·565	·562	·559
1·8	0·556	·552	·549	·546	·543	·541	·538	·535	·532	·529
1·9	0·526	·524	·521	·518	·515	·513	·510	·508	·505	·503
2·0	0·500	·498	·495	·493	·490	·488	·485	·483	·481	·478
2·1	0·476	·474	·472	·469	·467	·465	·463	·461	·459	·457
2·2	0·455	·452	·450	·448	·446	·444	·442	·441	·439	·437
2·3	0·435	·433	·431	·429	·427	·426	·424	·422	·420	·418
2·4	0·417	·415	·413	·412	·410	·408	·407	·405	·403	·402
2·5	0·400	·398	·397	·395	·394	·392	·391	·389	·388	·386
2·6	0·385	·383	·382	·380	·379	·377	·376	·375	·373	·372
2·7	0·370	·369	·368	·366	·365	·364	·362	·361	·360	·358
2·8	0·357	·356	·355	·353	·352	·351	·350	·348	·347	·346
2·9	0·345	·344	·342	·341	·340	·339	·338	·337	·336	·334
3·0	0·333	·332	·331	·330	·329	·328	·327	·326	·325	·324
3·1	0·323	·322	·321	·319	·318	·317	·316	·315	·314	·313
3·2	0·313	·312	·311	·310	·309	·308	·307	·306	·305	·304
3·3	0·303	·302	·301	·300	·299	·299	·298	·297	·296	·295
3·4	0·294	·293	·292	·292	·291	·290	·289	·288	·287	·287
3·5	0·286	·285	·284	·283	·282	·282	·281	·280	·279	·279
3·6	0·278	·277	·276	·275	·275	·274	·273	·272	·272	·271
3·7	0·270	·270	·269	·268	·267	·267	·266	·265	·265	·264
3·8	0·263	·262	·262	·261	·260	·260	·259	·258	·258	·257
3·9	0·256	·256	·255	·254	·254	·253	·253	·252	·251	·251
4·0	0·250	·249	·249	·248	·248	·247	·246	·246	·245	·244
4·1	0·244	·243	·243	·242	·242	·241	·240	·240	·239	·239
4·2	0·238	·238	·237	·236	·236	·235	·235	·234	·234	·233
4·3	0·233	·232	·231	·231	·230	·230	·229	·229	·228	·228
4·4	0·227	·227	·226	·226	·225	·225	·224	·224	·223	·223
4·5	0·222	·222	·221	·221	·220	·220	·219	·219	·218	·218
4·6	0·217	·217	·216	·216	·216	·215	·215	·214	·214	·213
4·7	0·213	·212	·212	·211	·211	·211	·210	·210	·209	·209
4·8	0·208	·208	·207	·207	·207	·206	·206	·205	·205	·204
4·9	0·204	·204	·203	·203	·202	·202	·202	·201	·201	·200
5·0	0·200	·200	·199	·199	·198	·198	·198	·197	·197	·196
5·1	0·196	·196	·195	·195	·195	·194	·194	·193	·193	·193
5·2	0·192	·192	·192	·191	·191	·190	·190	·190	·189	·189
5·3	0·189	·188	·188	·188	·187	·187	·187	·186	·186	·186
5·4	0·185	·185	·185	·184	·184	·183	·183	·183	·182	·182

RECIPROCALS

	0	1	2	3	4	5	6	7	8	9
5.5	0.182	.181	.181	.181	.181	.180	.180	.180	.179	.179
5.6	0.179	.178	.178	.178	.177	.177	.177	.176	.176	.176
5.7	0.175	.175	.175	.175	.174	.174	.174	.173	.173	.173
5.8	0.172	.172	.172	.172	.171	.171	.171	.170	.170	.170
5.9	0.169	.169	.169	.169	.168	.168	.168	.168	.167	.167
6.0	0.167	.166	.166	.166	.166	.165	.165	.165	.164	.164
6.1	0.164	.164	.163	.163	.163	.163	.162	.162	.162	.162
6.2	0.161	.161	.161	.161	.160	.160	.160	.159	.159	.159
6.3	0.159	.158	.158	.158	.158	.157	.157	.157	.157	.156
6.4	0.156	.156	.156	.156	.155	.155	.155	.155	.154	.154
6.5	0.154	.154	.153	.153	.153	.153	.152	.152	.152	.152
6.6	0.152	.151	.151	.151	.151	.150	.150	.150	.150	.149
6.7	0.149	.149	.149	.149	.148	.148	.148	.148	.147	.147
6.8	0.147	.147	.147	.146	.146	.146	.146	.146	.145	.145
6.9	0.145	.145	.145	.144	.144	.144	.144	.143	.143	.143
7.0	0.143	.143	.142	.142	.142	.142	.142	.141	.141	.141
7.1	0.141	.141	.140	.140	.140	.140	.140	.139	.139	.139
7.2	0.139	.139	.139	.138	.138	.138	.138	.138	.137	.137
7.3	0.137	.137	.137	.136	.136	.136	.136	.136	.136	.135
7.4	0.135	.135	.135	.135	.134	.134	.134	.134	.134	.134
7.5	0.133	.133	.133	.133	.133	.132	.132	.132	.132	.132
7.6	0.132	.131	.131	.131	.131	.131	.131	.130	.130	.130
7.7	0.130	.130	.130	.129	.129	.129	.129	.129	.129	.128
7.8	0.128	.128	.128	.128	.128	.127	.127	.127	.127	.127
7.9	0.127	.126	.126	.126	.126	.126	.126	.125	.125	.125
8.0	0.125	.125	.125	.125	.124	.124	.124	.124	.124	.124
8.1	0.123	.123	.123	.123	.123	.123	.123	.122	.122	.122
8.2	0.122	.122	.122	.122	.121	.121	.121	.121	.121	.121
8.3	0.120	.120	.120	.120	.120	.120	.120	.119	.119	.119
8.4	0.119	.119	.119	.119	.118	.118	.118	.118	.118	.118
8.5	0.118	.118	.117	.117	.117	.117	.117	.117	.117	.116
8.6	0.116	.116	.116	.116	.116	.116	.115	.115	.115	.115
8.7	0.115	.115	.115	.115	.114	.114	.114	.114	.114	.114
8.8	0.114	.114	.113	.113	.113	.113	.113	.113	.113	.112
8.9	0.112	.112	.112	.112	.112	.112	.112	.111	.111	.111
9.0	0.111	.111	.111	.111	.111	.110	.110	.110	.110	.110
9.1	0.110	.110	.110	.110	.109	.109	.109	.109	.109	.109
9.2	0.109	.109	.108	.108	.108	.108	.108	.108	.108	.108
9.3	0.108	.107	.107	.107	.107	.107	.107	.107	.107	.106
9.4	0.106	.106	.106	.106	.106	.106	.106	.106	.105	.105
9.5	0.105	.105	.105	.105	.105	.105	.105	.104	.104	.104
9.6	0.104	.104	.104	.104	.104	.104	.104	.103	.103	.103
9.7	0.103	.103	.103	.103	.103	.103	.102	.102	.102	.102
9.8	0.102	.102	.102	.102	.102	.102	.101	.101	.101	.101
9.9	0.101	.101	.101	.101	.101	.101	.100	.100	.100	.100
10.0	0.100									

FORMULAE

Length of arc of circle $\qquad l = r\theta$

Area of sector of circle $\qquad A = \frac{1}{2}r^2\theta$ $\qquad$ θ in radians

Trapezium rule for area under a curve

$$A \simeq \frac{h}{2}(y_1 + y_n + 2y_2 + 2y_3 + \ldots + 2y_{n-1})$$

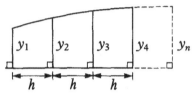

Volume of a right prism $\qquad V = Ah$

Volume of a right pyramid $\qquad V = \frac{1}{3}Ah$

Volume of a sphere $\qquad V = \frac{4}{3}\pi r^3$

Roots of quadratic equation $\qquad$ If $ax^2 + bx + c = 0,$

$$\text{then } x = \frac{-b \pm \sqrt{b^2 - 4ac}}{2a}$$

Standard deviation (ungrouped data)

$$s = \sqrt{\frac{\sum (x - \bar{x})^2}{n}}$$

$$= \sqrt{\frac{\sum x^2}{n} - \left(\frac{\sum x}{n}\right)^2}$$

Standard deviation (grouped data)

$$s = \sqrt{\frac{\sum fx^2}{n} - \left(\frac{\sum fx}{n}\right)^2}$$

where x is the mid-point of the class interval.

FORMULAE

Trigonometric ratios

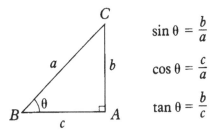

$$\sin \theta = \frac{b}{a}$$

$$\cos \theta = \frac{c}{a}$$

$$\tan \theta = \frac{b}{c}$$

$$\sin \theta = y$$

$$\cos \theta = x$$

$$\tan \theta = \frac{y}{x}$$

For $\triangle ABC \qquad \triangle = \frac{1}{2} ab \sin C$

$$= \sqrt{s(s-a)(s-b)(s-c)}$$

$$\frac{a}{\sin A} = \frac{b}{\sin B} = \frac{c}{\sin C}$$

$$a^2 = b^2 + c^2 - 2bc \cos A$$